Zentangle

of love and life

Akanksha Mishra

BookLeaf
Publishing

India | USA | UK

Presentation by *BookLeaf Publishing*

Web: www.bookleafpub.com

E-mail: info@bookleafpub.com

ISBN:9789360943684

First edition 2024

DEDICATION

To the readers, for giving this book their precious time.

And

To the people in my life, who didn't give up on me and have kept me motivated.

PREFACE

Dear Reader,

I have endeavored in this book, to give words and expression to the thoughts which are seldom spoken by us, or are dealt with by us within ourselves. Our deepest reflections either dwell in our dreams, fascinations, imaginations or remain suppressed at times. This book will fulfill its purpose if it has been able to ink even some of your feelings. May you find a piece of yourself expressed in the pages of this book.

Warm Regards
Akanksha Mishra

Eternal home

In millions of births,
and thousands of times,
we might stay far,
for days, months, years or even ages,
but I know,
our souls,
will always recognize their home,
whenever we pass by,
and,
would return to each other,
every time,
to finally rest in eternity…

Love potion

How much do I love you?
Or,
How much should I love you?
should I keep giving it all,
loving you in abstract,
pushing all my boundaries,
engulfed in you,
Fading and flurrying away in your love,
like a river in an ocean,
or should I look up to you,
waiting for your return,
and pour some love,
to refill mine,
and let them dissolve,
to create a new magic,
and make it endless,
and infinite beyond time...

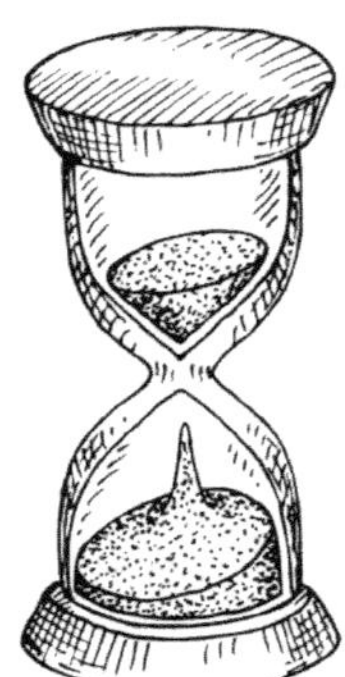

Vast as universe

I sit down,
to write,
what all my soul feels for you,
but I always get up,
after hours,
searching for words, phrases and rhymes,
But,
I end up having blank pages,
with not even a single word inked.

After all,
A piece of paper cannot sustain,
Love,
as vast as the Universe.

You all around

Sights, I can't watch,
without seeing you,
Songs, that I can't listen to,
without hearing you,
Days,
when even the sun,
the moon and the breeze,
surround me with you.
And there are moments,
when in every atom of my
existence,
I feel you.

Billions of people,
on this earth,
And yet my heart
chose you,
The world is an
illusion itself,
and yet,
my heart chose to live,
in the illusion of your love,
A thousand ways to live this life,
yet it chose to die every day,
longing and waiting,

to be embraced by you once,
Dreaming of you,
Knowing that you won't return...

When you're not here

I tell the stars,
and sing to the moon about you.
The words stay with me,
I hope the love reaches out to you.

The wind carries my heart,
and flies it to you,
I've sent my
warmth,
with the
sunshine,and I
hope,
those flowers give
you my smile,
just in time,
Oh, and don't
forget,
I've sent my soul with those clouds,
when it rains,
know that it's just for you.

I've thousands of words to say,
and a million feelings to express,
But I know,
the words will always stay with me,

I hope,
Love reaches out to you...

Show me your scars

Tell me,
Tell me, all of your stories,
Your fears, your insecurities,
and your heartaches,
and I would listen,
till you can smile again.

Show me,
your scars,
all the embers,
you had to walk upon,
and struggles,
you had to walk through,
and I will hold your hand,
till you heal,
and walk with you,
till the end of the road.

Tell me your dreams,
and I will build them with you,
and if you ever,
fall short of words,
share your silence,
and I will hear your heart...

It was always you

It was you, it always was you,
passing through me,
taking a heartbeat along,
skipping that one moment,
and sprinkling your magic in it,
But,
I could always only blame the moon,
and the cold breeze,
for showing my soul,
The eternity,
in the blink of a second...

Me, in You

Unable to differentiate,
between love and attachment,
Afraid,
of being and becoming somber,
While I care.
Juggling between,
Giving and draining myself out.
I've lost,
My own whereabouts.
Do me a favour,
Search for me, in you,
You may find in there,
echoes, of my laughter, shared with you,
Threads of love, I left with you,
Pieces of dreams,
That only we know about,
Help me find,
those memories,
To build myself again,
to cherish,
some more laughter,
to listen to a few more songs,
to see some more dreams,
To find it again,
What has been lost from us,

to live,
In each other,
Once again…

Pieces of me

Sometimes I wonder,
If you too had written,
pieces of me,
in your poems, letters,
Hidden, away from everyone else,
Kept safe in words,
Somewhere close to your heart.
I wonder,
If you too, find me,
In a song or a melody,
Or see me dancing, when it rains,
I wonder,
If a serendipitous thought of me,
Makes you smile, in the middle of your day,
I wonder
Whether your heart,
still remembers my love,
And if a piece of me
is still loved by you...

Barren heart

Everything you say or do,
Every time you look or touch,
My heart decodes it as love,
If, for you,
it was anything other than that,
then change mine,
with an empty dying heart,
barren of love…

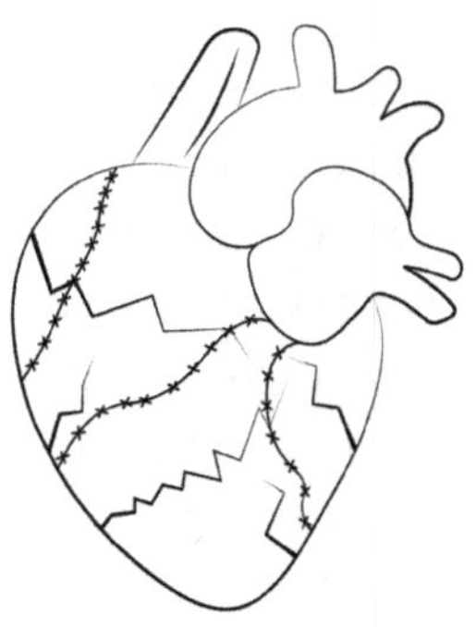

Fragile dream

It was a mistake,
To let you in,
To unravel my heart to you,
To let you dive into
The depths of me
And leave your traces in every bit of me,
I let you walk through,
my mornings and my darkest nights,
You saw,
the demons my heart fights,
I shared with you,
Every fantasy and every wound,
I poured into you, all of me,
I gave it all, yet again,
But you walked away,
as you had seen me broken,
You labelled me as fragile,
You just saw my autumns,
But forgot the springs,
which blossomed just for you,
I tried harder,
And harder yet again,
To keep you close
And I would still take any pain,
But you've turned your back now,

And all I could see was,
you going further away,
I still feel you all around every day,
But it's just my dream,
Which will fade far away…

Parallel lives

Does it take courage?
or is it cowardice?
to be silent,
when all we want is to scream our minds out.
Is it helplessness?
or is it being selfish?
To mask a happy face,
On a crying, scarred heart.
Is it being wise or crippled?
To not gorge the decisions we actually discord,
Just to keep peace with the ones we care for,
Is it called living or dying?
To live two different lives at once and all the
time.

The last one standing

Let my heart be broken,
not once,
not twice,
but innumerable times.
and still bleed love.
let me witness,
the annihilation love brings,
Let my existence be shattered,
a million times,
Yet blossom with love,
Let my soul become an ocean,
In which all the pain, suffering, loss,
fear and obliteration of the universe,
will feel as small as an atom.
Let me experience,
and go right through the hellfire,
and bury all my desires in peace
and set me free for eternity...

One Day

One day,
all this will make sense,
one day,
the barriers will fall,
and I will rise,
with all the might,
yet calm, beautiful and wise.
one day,
it will all fall into place,
and the life will shine,
with a golden grace,
one day,
there'll be no chase,
and dreams will turn real
one day,
nothing will be put to test,
all the hurries and worries will come to rest,
one day,
there'll be magic around,
and the truth shall be found,
one day,
the mind will see the unseen,
and I'll be there where I have never been,
one day,
the wounds will be healed,

and the mysteries be revealed,
the mind will be calm,
and the soul be infinite,
all of this,
will make sense...one day...

Metaphysical love

You entered my life,
like a neutron star,
magnetic,
pulling me in your gravity,
engulfing me,
from inside out,
And I could feel,
a thousand galaxies colliding,
And exploding,
with the untouched,
unearthed emotions of my heart,

You brought the magic,
Of a whole new universe,
And a hundred suns shined within me,
Enchanting,
And filled with life,
Surrounded with,
a divine, mesmerizing sea of stars,
and making me a part of you
with every wave…

The light within

Sitting on a skerry,
under the silvery stars,
on a greyish night of life,
when everything seems far,

When your demons grow up on you,
with their talons piercing your flesh,
when it's you against you,
yet you're alone in this clash,

When everything seems to be falling apart,
and you can barely hear your heart,
when even the moon looks pale,
and darkness is all that prevails,

Surrender,
Surrender and remember,
to call for your soul,

or your mind and your heart,
can be manipulated and won over,
they can always be torn apart,

But the soul,
it's fire,
endless, timeless and pure.

Let it pave your way,
and see the flowers bloom,
with every step you take.

Surrender,
and let your soul be the shield,
and watch the darkness fade away
and your demons burnt to ashes.

So surrender,
and let the darkness be,
don't be afraid and you don't have to fight,
for you have a whole burning sun inside...

Word War

What are words?
Do they express?
or mostly used to impress?

Do they say feelings?
or do they deceive?
and cleverly hide them?

words can kill,
like wild hounds,
But if sprinkled with love,
they can heal bleeding wounds,

Are words swords?
or are they shields?
Are they weapons?
If so,
What power do they wield?

Are words better than silence?
Aren't lies lived in words,
but buried in silence.
Aren't words a deception?
to conceal the truths,
silence may reveal...

Does love need fortune?

I met a fortune teller today,
looking deep into her cards,
with her fingers moving,
And trying to catch their magic,

She told me
that you'll leave me,
torn and apart, someday,
with a goodbye,
wrapped in flowers and hearts,
with a heartache disguised as love,
a one-sided yearning,
to see that love and magic in your eyes,
And that I would lose my sanity,
longing for you.

But I wonder,
what little did she know of love,
does love need any sanity?

can love even be felt with intelligence?
Or is love meant to truly engulf,
Our individual existence,
and dissolve us into itself,
leaving no trace of us,
and yet filling us with its magic and warmth.
Maybe, what she couldn't see,
Was that,
I see you every day,
and still wait for you,
I talk to you even in silence,
feel you in every moment,
and yet,
I lose you every day.

I wonder if her cards told her,
that I still see, a little something in your eyes,
And feel the warmth in your voice,
That I still believe,
that wherever you are,
I am there in your heart,
and you too have loved me,
from the very start.

Did she see,
That I am drowned and saved,
by this love every day,
That love,
surrounds us with its music,

and yet leaves a dead silence within us,
That love,
Does it even need a fortune?
or is it the fortune itself?
Does it need a path?
Or is it the path itself?
I doubt,
And I wonder,
Did she ever know love in this way?

Moon child

Unfettered,
She dances on her own tunes,
She breathes magic,
and flows with the wind.

But she too was chained once,
she too,
had fought her own wars,
She wears them like a jewelled crown,
her ruby red scars,

She dreams of meadows, willows,
flowers and lilies,
and her eyes twinkle,
like a thousand fireflies,

She walks on the ocean of stars,
and carries a river of moonlight,
and galaxies in her heart.

Her soul,
made of fire,
Too pure to be touched,
Too wild to be tamed,
She shines like a Sun,

But,
She's a moon child,
if she ever will be named....

Thread of Fate

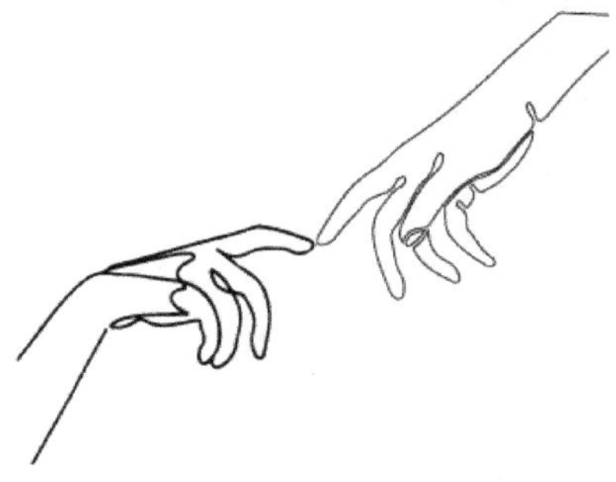

"Legend says,
two souls,
destined to be together,
are tied with red,
invisible thread,
unbreakable,
beyond space and time,
Irresistible to fates,
which are bound to meet each other,
in their lifetime." He told her.

Unaware,
That she already was intertwined,
in the threads of his love,
woven in and around her,
like arteries and veins,
pumping life into her heart.

And looking at their hands,
meeting and then drifting apart,
She wondered,
what destiny was engraved,
for their souls...

Bon voyage

When death knocks at your door,
and whispers in your ear,
"Now, is the time dear".
and you'll have no choice,
but to leave,
With no tickets, no luggage,
no see-offs and no goodbyes.

Will you yearn to hold on?

For a few moments more,
to say those words of love,
still locked in your heart,
waiting and wanting to be told.

To wipe those dreams,
flowing from your eyes,
which were meant to be chased, "Someday".

Or would you take a while,
to remember,
promises waiting to be kept,
those breakfasts, dinners and laughter,
which are yet to be planned.

That one letter,
which was never sent,
and that dance in the rain,
which was never danced.

Will you hold on some more?
to grieve in regret,
missing all the life,
while life was being managed.

But now,
the journey has come to an end,
everything and everyone is to be left behind,
but this baggage will have to be hauled.
heavy and painful enough,
to tear you apart.

Or,
Will you welcome with open arms,
and embrace the angel of death,
like a beloved.

Will you be mesmerized,
with the hues of dawn,
where life and death have reunited,
to celebrate,
your adventure till now.
A roller coaster ride, lively
and filled with precious moments and memories,

shining bright in time,
now to be left behind,
only to begin a new one.

With your heart,
as light as a feather,
but filled with peace and gratitude,
Will you choose,
to look into the eyes of death,
and say, "Bon Voyage"?